MW01231266

A Robbie Reader

Gardening For Kids

Organic Gardening for Kids

Elizabeth Scholl

Mitchell Lane
PUBLISHERS

P.O. Box 196
Hockessin, Delaware 19707
Visit us on the web: www.mitchelllane.com
Comments? email us; mitchelllane@mitchelllane.com

Mitchell Lane
PUBLISHERS

Gardening For Kids

A Backyard Flower Garden for Kids
A Backyard Vegetable Garden for Kids
Design Your Own Butterfly Garden
Design Your Own Pond and Water Garden
A Kid's Guide to Container Gardening
A Kid's Guide to Landscape Design
A Kid's Guide to Making a Terrarium
A Kid's Guide to Perennial Gardens
Organic Gardening for Kids

Copyright © 2010 by Mitchell Lane Publishers

All rights reserved. No part of this book may be reproduced without written permission from the publisher. Printed and bound in the United States of America.

PUBLISHER'S NOTE: The facts on which the story in this book is based have been thoroughly researched. Documentation of such research can be found on page 46. While every possible effort has been made to ensure accuracy, the publisher will not assume liability for damages caused by inaccuracies in the data, and makes no warranty on the accuracy of the information contained herein.

The insects shown on the running heads are beneficial to gardens because they hunt harmful insects: cryptolaemus beetle (chapter 1); lacewing larva (chapter 2); ladybug (chapter 3); praying mantis (chapter 4); spine soldier bug, also known as the stink bug (chapter 5).

ABOUT THE AUTHOR: Elizabeth Scholl has been an organic gardener for almost twenty years. She is certified by the National Wildlife Federation as a Habitat Steward, and helped establish an organic garden known as a schoolyard habitat, which provides food, water, cover, and a place to raise young for local wildlife at an elementary school.

Elizabeth is a writer of children's educational materials. She has published many books and articles on gardening, nature, and environmental topics.

When not writing and gardening, Elizabeth enjoys reading, hiking, watching birds and other wildlife, and bicycling. She lives in Northern New Jersey with her husband, three children, dog, and two very mischievous cats.

Library of Congress Cataloging-in-Publication Data
Scholl, Elizabeth J.
  Organic gardening for kids / by Elizabeth Scholl.
       p. cm. — (A Robbie reader. Gardening for kids)
  Includes bibliographical references and index.
  ISBN 978-1-58415-815-8 (library bound)
  1. Organic gardening—Juvenile literature.
I. Title. II. Series: Robbie reader. Gardening for kids.
  SB453.5.S36 2009
  635'.0484—dc22
                                              2009001317

Printing   2   3   4   5   6   7   8   9

PLB / PLB2

Contents

Words in **bold** type can be found in the glossary.

Introduction

Are you interested in planting a garden, or working in one that has already been planted? Perhaps you like the idea of working in nature—growing living things and spending time outdoors where you can be with the trees, birds, small animals, and insects.

Surprisingly, people often work against nature to grow a garden. When they see insects nibbling on their plants, they spray poisonous **insecticide** (in-SEK-tih-syd) to kill them. They spray **herbicide** (ER-bih-syd) to kill the weeds that grow between their plants. They put **fertilizers** (FER-tuh-ly-zerz) full of **chemicals** (KEH-mih-kulz) in the ground to make their plants grow bigger.

Some people grow beautiful flower gardens and harvest lots of vegetables using these methods.

Unfortunately, they are polluting the earth, air, and water.

Organic (or-GAA-nik) gardening is all about creating a balance with nature. Organic gardeners grow healthy plants without using chemicals. They put **nutrients** (NOO-tree-untz) back into the soil, so the earth remains healthy and **fertile** (FER-tul). They make sure animals, plants, and water systems—like rivers and oceans—are not harmed.

Before planting any type of garden, talk to your parent or guardian about your ideas. Make sure you have permission before you dig in your yard. You may want to ask for help and advice from an adult who has gardening experience. It is also nice to have company when you are working in your garden, and someone with whom to share your excitement when you see your plants growing.

Chapter
Chapter

1

Why Become an Organic Gardener?

You've probably heard something about organic food, or seen the word *organic* on labels. What does it mean if something is organic? It means it comes from living things. Organic food is grown without chemical fertilizers and pesticides. Instead, organic matter such as **compost** (KOM-pohst) made from decayed food and plants is used to add nutrients to the soil. Nutrients help plants grow strong, which helps them resist attacks by insects and diseases.

Why avoid using chemicals in your garden? People began using chemicals to grow plants when they had to grow large amounts of food. Because there are so many people in the world, and all those people need to eat, large crops must be grown efficiently. To keep away insects and diseases that damage crops, scientists developed chemicals that would kill the insects or stop plant diseases. Chemical fertilizers were created to feed the plants and make them grow larger and faster. However, too many chemicals are harmful. When chemicals like **nitrogen** (NY-troh-jin) get into rivers and lakes, the **ecosystems** (EE-koh-sis-tems) there become unbalanced. So much **algae** (AL-jee) grows, it uses up the oxygen that fish and other aquatic life need to live.

The first chemical pesticide to be used widely was called DDT. In 1939, when DDT was developed, it seemed like a very effective solution against crop pests. It was the first pesticide that could kill hundreds of different kinds of insects, including mosquitoes that caused malaria and lice that caused typhus, both deadly diseases. However, when rain carried DDT into the oceans, it killed seaweed and fish.

Frogs tell us when water is polluted, because they absorb poisonous chemicals through their skin. The frog on the left is healthy, while the one on the right has been in water polluted with DDT.

A scientist named Rachel Carson discovered that DDT also affected birds. Birds exposed to the toxin laid eggs with very thin shells. The shells were not strong enough to protect the unborn baby birds. Peregrine falcons, bald eagles, brown pelicans, and other species became endangered as a result of DDT use. DDT is now illegal to use in the United States, but it is still used in some other countries.

When large amounts of fertilizer are used on farms, some of it can be washed into rivers when it rains. The fertilizer can make so much algae grow that the waters become clogged. When the algae dies and decomposes, the process uses oxygen that river plants and animals need to live.

Organic gardeners work with nature, rather than against it. They grow healthy gardens that are safe for the environment. You can grow an organic garden anywhere —from a backyard to an apartment terrace to a patch of earth at your school. Organic gardening methods can be used to grow beautiful flowers, tasty vegetables and fruits, or herbs for a soothing tea or a spicy sauce.

By becoming an organic gardener, you will truly have

Garden Tip

A great way to begin planning your organic garden is to visit as many gardens as you can. These can be the gardens of friends, relatives, and neighbors, community or school gardens, or a botanical garden, if there is one nearby. The more gardens you see, the more inspired you will be to create your own beautiful garden.

a green thumb—because organic gardens help make the world a greener place. Your garden won't pollute the earth, air, or water with chemicals. You will learn how to select certain plants, as well as combinations of plants, that will attract helpful insects to your garden, and repel insects that could become pests.

Organic gardens even provide food, shelter, and a place for wildlife to raise their young, including birds, butterflies and other insects, worms, frogs, and toads. While the habitat of many animals is being developed into housing, office complexes,

You can plant your organic garden right in the ground (front of picture), or you can build raised beds (bordered with wood). Raised beds are useful for growing plants in low areas of a yard that tend to stay soggy after it rains. They can also be fenced to prevent animals such as rabbits and groundhogs from munching on your veggies. Fewer weeds grow in raised beds than in beds that are directly on the ground.

and shopping malls, your organic garden will be a small ecosystem for them. In return, they will help you by making your soil healthier, eating unwanted pests, and **pollinating** (PAH-lih-nay-ting) your plants. In short, organic gardening is helpful to everyone.

Chapter
Chapter
2

Sun, Water, and Soil

Many schoolchildren plant beans or flower seeds and watch them grow in science class. If you have done this, you know that plants need three things to grow: light, water, and soil.

The amount of sun your garden gets will greatly affect what plants grow well there. If you have a location that is shady, you will need to choose plants that prefer less light. While a very sunny spot is often considered ideal for a flower or vegetable garden, don't be discouraged if your area is partly shady or even very shady. There are many varieties of flowers, herbs, and even some vegetables that will be happy and thrive in places where the sun is not beating down on them all day. In this chapter, you will learn how to choose the best plants for the amount of sun your garden receives.

Water is also essential to a garden. How easy will it be for you to water your garden? Most gardens need to be watered regularly, especially right after seeds have been planted or young plants are bursting out of the soil. When the sun is hot, soil dries out fast. Make sure you can get to your water source easily. If it is hard to get water to your plants, you may lose enthusiasm

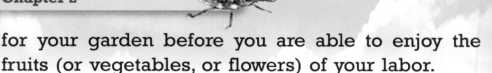

for your garden before you are able to enjoy the fruits (or vegetables, or flowers) of your labor.

Even though plants need water, you should try to choose a level spot where the soil drains easily for your garden. A low spot, such as the bottom of a hill, may remain soggy for a long time after it rains. Too much moisture will keep some plants from getting enough oxygen from the soil. However, if the only spot for your garden looks like a swamp after it rains, and you can't build raised beds, Mother Nature can still help you. There are plants that actually like soggy conditions. Plants have adapted to all sorts of areas, and some grow in or near marshy or wetland areas.

Garden Tip

To find out the texture of your soil, take some moist soil from your garden and squeeze it into a ball. If you open your hand and it crumbles, you have sandy soil. If the soil stays in a ball when you open your hand, but crumbles when you poke it, you are lucky. Your soil is a good texture for plants. If your ball of soil doesn't crumble even when poked, you have clay soil.

An organic gardener never refers to soil as *dirt,* which sometimes means something unwanted or worthless. To the organic gardener, soil is valuable and needs to be nurtured just as plants do. Your plants will be getting food from the soil. The more nutritious (noo-TRIH-shus) the food in the soil, the healthier the plants will be.

Soil is made up partly of finely ground rocks and minerals, and partly of organic matter. Organic matter is the remains of dead plants and animals in the process of **decomposing** (dee-kum-POH-zing). Soil also contains oxygen and water.

Soil provides a home to millions of living **organisms**—both plants and animals. Some you can see, like worms, and some can only be seen with a microscope. These living beings provide food for plants, and also improve the quality of the

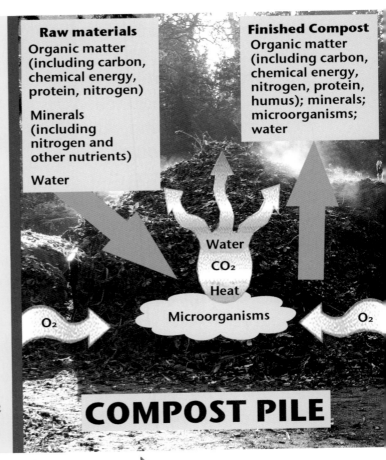

During composting, microorganisms eat the organic waste, breaking it down to its simplest parts. This is done through a process called respiration, which requires air and water. When you turn or mix your compost bin, you provide the air needed for respiration. The microorganisms give off carbon dioxide and heat, creating finished compost in a few weeks or months.

Raw materials
Organic matter (including carbon, chemical energy, protein, nitrogen)

Minerals (including nitrogen and other nutrients)

Water

Finished Compost
Organic matter (including carbon, chemical energy, nitrogen, protein, humus); minerals; microorganisms; water

Water
CO_2
Heat
Microorganisms
O_2
O_2

COMPOST PILE

soil by breaking it up as they travel around.

It is important to know what type of soil your garden has, as this will help you determine what plants will grow best there. Some soil is acidic (ah-SIH-dik), and some is alkaline (AL-kuh-lyn). The amount of acid or alkaline in the soil is called the pH. You can buy a pH kit at a garden center and test your soil at home, or bring a bag of soil to a garden center and let them test the pH for you. The pH scale ranges from 0 to 14. Soil right in the middle, measuring 7, is neutral. Soil that measures lower than 7 is more acidic. Soil that measures higher than 7 is more alkaline. Most garden plants prefer soil that is slightly acidic. On

Testing your soil for pH will help you choose the plants that will grow well in your soil type. You can test it yourself with a pH soil tester kit. A sample of dry soil is put into a container, and water with a special liquid, powder, or strip of paper is added. The water or paper strip turns a color, which when matched with colors on a pH chart tells you how acidic or alkaline your soil is.

Much of your kitchen garbage can be recycled to make compost, which is very nutritious for your garden. Coffee grounds, banana peels, onion skins, apple cores, and eggshells are all great ingredients for a compost pile or bin. Keeping a container under the sink just for compost makes it easy to carry the goodies outdoors to your composter.

the other hand, desert plants thrive in very alkaline soil.

When soil is too acidic or too alkaline, plants can't absorb certain nutrients they need from the soil, so they don't grow well. You can change the pH of your soil by adding different organic ingredients. For example, limestone will make acidic soil more alkaline. Dried leaves or pine needles will make alkaline soil more acidic. Changing your soil's pH in these ways is temporary, and eventually the soil will go back to its original pH. Adding compost to any type of soil is an organic gardener's best choice. Compost **neutralizes** (NOO-truh-ly-zez) both acidic and alkaline soils—bringing them closer to a 7 on the pH scale. It adds nutrients to the soil as well.

Plants That Grow Well in Acidic Soil	
Acidic Soil	Sun/Shade
blueberries	sun
eggplant	sun
lilies	sun
potatoes	sun
primrose	part sun to shade
strawberries	sun
wax begonias	part shade to shade
woodland phlox	part sun

You also need to know the texture of your soil— whether it is sandy or clay. While some plants can grow in sandy soil and some in clay, most soils will

Plants That Grow Well in Alkaline Soil

Alkaline Soil	Sun/Shade
clematis	full sun
dwarf baby's breath	sun
nasturtiums	sun to part sun
oregano	sun
pinchusion flowers	full sun
salvia	sun to part sun
speedwell	full sun
zinnias	sun

benefit from some improvement. Trying to dig into hard, dry clay is not easy, nor is working with wet, sticky clay. A very sandy soil does not hold water well and has to be watered often.

All types of soil can be greatly improved by adding nutrients. Instead of using chemical fertilizers, organic gardeners use organic matter, such as horse, chicken, or cow manure and bone meal. (Processed bone meal is best, since fish bones can attract unwanted animals to the garden, and shouldn't be used in compost piles for that reason.) **Guano**, or bird droppings, and compost are very good for gardens. Besides adding nutrients, compost improves the texture of your soil, making it easier to work with. You can buy compost at a garden center, but many organic gardeners make their own compost.

Espoma
SINCE 1929
Organic Traditions™

ALL NATURAL ORGANIC

Bone Meal
Pure Source of Phosphorus
Promotes Root & Flower Growth

Chapter
Chapter

3

What Should I Plant?

What type of garden will you plant? You may be interested in an ornamental flower garden. Perhaps you want to grow vegetables, fruits, or herbs you can eat.

Whether you want flowers or food or both, it is best to choose plants that need the amount of sun your garden has, grow well in your soil type, and are generally easy to grow. This is a good recipe for a successful garden.

Designing Your Garden

In addition to deciding what to plant, you will need to determine how to arrange your plants in your garden space. This is a fun and creative part of gardening.

There are many options for the design of your garden, but there are a few rules to follow that will help your garden look its best, especially if you are growing flowers and other decorative plants. One is putting taller plants in the back of your garden and smaller ones in the front, so the tall ones don't hide the short ones. Another is planting both **annuals** and **perennials**, because while your perennials will bloom for only a few weeks, annuals will stay in bloom the whole season, always providing color to your garden.

You can get some ideas about garden design by looking at gardens in your neighborhood, or by looking at pictures of gardens in books and magazines. Think about color combinations in addition to sizes. If you are planting flowers, you probably won't want all purple ones, even if purple is your favorite color.

The size, shape, and color of plants all add to the design of your garden. Think about the shape and size of the leaves as well as of the flowers. For variety and an interesting landscape, mix pointy posies with rounder, fuller flowers, and make sure larger plants don't hide small and medium-sized plants.

Choosing the Best Plants for your Garden

There are eleven planting zones in the United States and southern Canada. The higher the zone number, the warmer the temperatures in that zone. Knowing your planting zone can help you choose the right plants for your climate, as well as the time of year it becomes warm enough to begin planting.

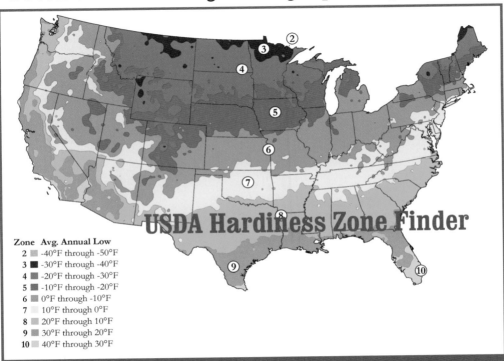

Zone Avg. Annual Low
2 -40°F through -50°F
3 -30°F through -40°F
4 -20°F through -30°F
5 -10°F through -20°F
6 0°F through -10°F
7 10°F through 0°F
8 20°F through 10°F
9 30°F through 20°F
10 40°F through 30°F

The United States is divided into hardiness zones. (Not pictured are Alaska, in Zone 1, and Hawaii, in Zone 11.) These zones are based on average winter temperature. Before choosing plants for your garden, you should know the hardiness zone of the area in which you live. Only choose plants that are known to grow well in your hardiness zone.

See the chart on the next page for a few suggestions for plants that grow well in all planting regions. These are also easy to grow if planted in the right place, with the right conditions.

Most vegetables need full sun; beans, lettuces, and most other leafy greens can tolerate part shade. No vegetables do well in full shade.

Easy-to-Grow Vegetables

carrots   cucumbers   green beans

lettuce   peas   radishes

sweet peppers   tomatoes   zucchini

An herb garden can provide a number of things: flavorings for cooking, attractive flowering plants, healing potions, delicious teas, and fragrant **potpourris** (poh-por-EEZ). Some herbs, such as parsley, are also very attractive to butterflies.

	Perennials		Annuals	
Sun	coreopsis		chrysanthemum	
	pinchusion flower		cosmo	
	purple coneflower		marigold	
	salvia		nasturtium	
	yarrow		zinnia	
Shade	astilbe		begonia	
	bleeding heart		browallia	
	columbine		impatiens	
	hosta		nicotiana	
	primrose		torenia	
	trillium		viola	

Most herbs like a lot of sun. Herbs that are easy to grow and that are used regularly include:

basil   chamomile   chives   lavender

mint   oregano   parsley

If your garden area does not drain well and is soggy, you will have the most success with wetland plants, which naturally grow near streams or in and around swamps. These plants will do well in sun to partial shade. Some suggestions are:

arrowhead   bee balm   cardinal flower   fern

goldenrod   joe-pye weed   marsh marigold   swamp milkweed

These plants—for dry, sandy soil—prefer sunny conditions:

blanket flower false indigo portulaca sedum

sunflower yarrow yucca zinnia

Here are some plants that can help each other if planted together. This is called companion planting:

Borage repels many pests, and is helpful
   when planted with tomatoes, cucumbers,
   strawberries, and most other plants
Chives help prevent **aphids**
   from attacking lettuces
Garlic helps keep away rabbits when
   planted with lettuce, peas, and cucumbers
Marigolds deter **Mexican bean beetles**
   from eating the leaves and young
   pods of bean plants

Nasturtiums planted with squash keep
squash bugs and beetles away
Rosemary repels **carrot flies**

Mapping It Out

Drawing a map can help you plan your garden.
Draw the border of your garden space. Add the
trees, bushes, buildings, fences, and any other
objects that will remain in the area. Make sure you

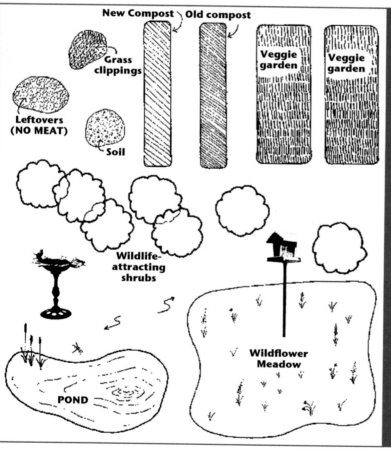

New Compost · Old compost

Grass clippings

Veggie garden · Veggie garden

Leftovers (NO MEAT)

Soil

Wildlife-attracting shrubs

Wildflower Meadow

POND

You don't have to be a great artist to create a diagram or picture of your garden-to-be. Plotting your garden on paper will not only help you see what will fit and look good in different areas, it will also help you remember what plants you planted and where.

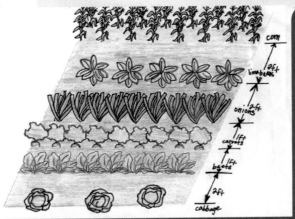

Garden Tip

If you don't have a yard, you can plant a container garden. Use the same guidelines for the amount of sunlight and water, and the type of soil. Then choose plants that won't grow very large. You can move your container outdoors during nice weather, then bring it inside for the winter.

A diagram can help you figure out the best way to organize your plants so that your garden will flourish. Follow the directions on the seed packet or seedling pot to determine how many rows you can have, and how many plants in each row.

create a path or two, so you will have access to your plants for watering and tending. You can also draw objects you might like to add, like a birdbath or birdfeeder. Draw your plants in the arrangement you imagine, with taller ones in the back and shorter ones in the front of your garden.

Drawing your garden and keeping a journal will also let you look back on your records when you are planning next year's garden. It will help you decide what you will keep the same way, and what you will change.

Chapter

Chapter

4

Creating Your Organic Garden

Now that you've made your plans, you are ready to garden. First, gather a few basic tools. You may want to choose ones that are made for children, as regular tools may be too large or too heavy to work with easily. Here are some useful ones:

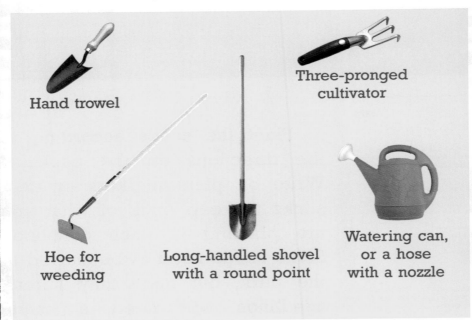

Hand trowel

Three-pronged cultivator

Hoe for weeding

Long-handled shovel with a round point

Watering can, or a hose with a nozzle

Getting a Head Start

If you have space indoors and good lighting, you can get a head start before warm weather comes by starting seeds indoors. For this project you will need:

- Seeds
- Potting soil or seed-starting mix (a special kind of soil specifically for starting plants from seeds)
- Small containers such as egg cartons, or seed trays from a garden store
- A spoon for scooping small amounts of soil into containers
- Plant markers (or craft sticks) and a permanent marker to label your containers
- A sunny window or a fluorescent light

Plant the seeds according to the directions on the package. Write on plant markers or craft sticks to keep track of what you are planting in each container. Some seeds need to be started in the dark, but once they sprout, seedlings will need a sunny window to thrive. If you don't have a sunny windowsill, seedlings will grow quite well under fluorescent lights, but they need to be very close to the light—the light should be three to six inches above the

Starting seeds indoors is an easy and inexpensive way to start your garden, and it also allows you to begin before it warms up enough to plant outdoors.

plants. If you have a shop light in your basement, or if you can talk your parents into investing in a fluorescent light fixture with long tube bulbs (they can be bought for as little as $10), you can start your own small indoor plant nursery. Be sure to use long bulbs; the curlicue fluorescent bulbs made for everyday lamps are too small if you want to start a lot of seeds.

If starting seeds inside doesn't work for you, it is fine to wait until it warms up enough outside to plant seeds directly into the ground. Another idea is to buy small plants to plant in the ground or in containers. Many supermarkets, home centers, and garden centers carry flower, herb, and vegetable seedlings in the spring.

Before you plant your seeds or seedlings, you will need to till, or loosen, the soil so that the plants can be put in the ground easily. This should be done when the ground is warm (at least 60 degrees) and dry. The soil is warm enough to till if you can stick your finger a few inches down into it and keep it there comfortably for a minute. To see if the soil is dry enough, pick up some soil and try to squeeze it into a ball in your hand. If it falls apart when you poke it, the soil is dry enough, and you can begin to till.

With your cultivator, work in rows and loosen the top few inches of soil. One tilling per row is enough—over-tilling can cause the soil to compact, instead of loosening it. If your soil is clay or sandy, add about an inch of compost to your garden bed, and mix it into the loosened soil. This will help the soil's texture and add nutrients.

You are now ready to put your seeds or plants in the ground. If you are planting seedlings, be very

Garden Tip

Create a garden journal. As your garden grows, write down which plants are doing well, which ones are not, methods you find that are helpful, and things you would like to do differently in the future. Take photos of your garden for your journal, or spend time in your garden drawing your plants. You can also write down the names of plants that you might like to grow next year. You may think you will remember everything for next year's garden, but chances are, you will forget things if you don't write them down.

Tilling the soil is usually done in the spring, once the soil has warmed up and is not too wet. If you have a small garden area, you can loosen the soil with a three-pronged cultivator. If your garden is larger, you will probably want to use a long-handled shovel or rake.

gentle when removing them from their containers. Tapping the container lightly will loosen the plant and make it easier to take out. Hold the plant by the roots or the base of its stem. Picking up a plant by the leaves can cause its stem to break. For seedlings, dig holes, and put the plants in gently.

The fun part about planting seedlings or starter plants is that you can see what your garden is going to look like as soon as you put the plants in, without having to wait for the seeds to sprout.

Watering your garden regularly is an essential part of gardening. Make sure your seeds or plants are well watered, but not soaked. Seeds and young plants must be kept moist, so you may need to water every day unless it rains.

Then pack the soil around them firmly enough to keep the plant in place. If you are planting seeds, follow the package directions.

Once you've planted your seedlings or seeds, water them thoroughly. If you use a hose, make sure you use a nozzle with a gentle spray—too strong of a spray can wash seeds out of the ground or break the stems of young plants.

Congratulations! Your organic garden has been planted. With regular care and maintenance, like watering, weeding, and preventing unwanted pests, your plants will soon be flourishing.

Chapter 5

Chapter

Maintaining Your Organic Garden

Even if you plant companion plants to help control pests, your organic garden can suffer from weeds and insects just as easily as non-organic gardens. If you want to avoid using chemical herbicides and pesticides, how can you keep your garden safe and thriving?

Weeds

The first tool an organic gardener uses to combat weeds is a layer of organic **mulch** three to four inches thick. Mulch made of shredded bark, straw, chopped leaves (leaves can be chopped with a lawn mower **by an adult**), wood chips, or grass clippings will prevent weeds from growing by blocking their sunlight. To make an even stronger barrier against weeds, you can put a layer of newspaper, cardboard, or brown paper grocery bags underneath the mulch. Mulch is also beneficial because it helps keep moisture in the ground, and as it decomposes, it adds nutrients to your soil.

Another way to stop weeds from taking over is to cut them with a hoe. Hoeing works best when the weeds are just coming up and are still small. Scrape the top inch or so of the soil with your hoe, cutting the stems of the weeds with the blade. You can leave the cut weeds on the ground to decompose.

If your weeds have grown larger, or if it is difficult to hoe without damaging your plants, you can pull the weeds out by hand. Grab the weed at the base of the stem, near the ground. Wiggle the stem a bit to loosen it, and pull gently, so the root will come

Weeds will crowd out your plants and use up the nutrients in the soil, so it is important to control them. Though weeding can be a lot of work, when you are finished, you can step back and admire how nice your garden looks.

out. If the weeds have gone to seed, or have seeds on them, throw them away, or you will have more weeds growing from the seeds. Otherwise, you can leave the plants on the ground to decompose. If it is a very tough plant to pull out, such as a dandelion, you may need to use your trowel to dig the root out of the ground.

Insects

You've paired your plants with their beneficial companions to keep pests away. You've added compost to your soil to make the plants strong and resistant to harmful insects. Yet you are still having problems with insects attacking your plants. Now what?

First of all, observe what the insects are doing. If insects are munching on your plant leaves a bit, but the plant still looks healthy, you may not really have an insect problem. If you find out that your plants are being attacked and damaged by insects, there are some methods that organic gardeners use that don't harm people, animals, the environment, or insects other than the ones you are trying to get rid of.

Before you attempt to get rid of your garden pests, you must identify them. There are a number of environmentally friendly products you can buy, including oils and sprays, that will repel or kill garden pests. Different methods work for different species of insects. Insect traps are also available. These attract particular kinds of insects onto colored sticky paper, which you can then throw away.

Many organic gardeners use homemade remedies to deter insects. For example, putting crushed eggshells around the base of plants will keep slugs and snails away, because they don't like the sharp edges of the eggshells. Cayenne pepper and garlic repel many insects, as well as rabbits and other animals. You can try the homemade recipe on page 43. It will repel aphids, beetles, caterpillars, spider mites, and whiteflies.

Another method of getting rid of unwanted insects is to invite predators of those insects into your garden. Ladybugs eat aphids, whiteflies, spider mites, and mealybugs. Some garden centers sell live, adult ladybugs, and they are available for purchase on the web at many online garden supply stores. Praying mantises, which are also predatory, will eat aphids, beetles, grasshoppers, and caterpillars. You can buy praying mantis egg cases that contain a few hundred praying mantis eggs, and these will hatch in your garden.

It is important to be consistent about taking care of your garden. Visit it as often as you can. It is much easier to pull out a few weeds every day than to

RECIPE

Garlic and Cayenne Pepper
Insect Repellent

Ingredients	Supplies
6 garlic cloves, peeled	Blender or food processor (have an adult help you)
1 tablespoon cayenne pepper	Jar or container (one quart or larger) with lid
1 tablespoon biodegradable	Strainer
dishwashing liquid (not detergent)	Spray bottle
4 cups water	

Put garlic, cayenne pepper, dishwashing liquid, and one cup of water in a food processor or blender. Blend until smooth. Pour the mixture into a jar or container.

Add the other three cups of water. Put on the cover. Let stand for twenty-four hours.

Strain the liquid into the spray bottle. Spray on the affected plants.

You will need to reapply this mixture after it rains.

wait several weeks until you have a garden full of weeds. It is also much easier to control an insect problem when it begins on just one or two plants than to wait until your garden is infested with pests.

The more care you put into your organic garden, the more pleasure you will get from it. You will be proud of your garden because it will be a source of delicious healthy food or beautiful flowers, as well as a habitat for many small creatures. When you plant an organic garden, you are making a promise to protect and care for the planet.

Craft

Build a Worm Composter

Worm composting, also known as **vermiculture** (VER-mih-kul-chur), is a great way to turn waste into usable soil. It can be done even if you live in an apartment and have no place to make compost outside. You can make a worm composter in a plastic storage bin, and it allows you to turn most of your family's food scraps, which would normally be trash, into high-quality compost. If you care for your worm bin properly, within about six months, you will have rich, fertile soil for your plants.

You Will Need

An adult to help you

Two plastic storage bins with lids (**not** the see-through type)—you can use an 8-gallon to 10-gallon size, or larger if you have the space

Hand or power drill with 1/4-inch and 1/16-inch drill bits—use only with adult supervision

Newspaper, shredded into 1-inch strips—do not use glossy paper

Bucket

Handful of leaves or soil

One pound of red worms. It is best to order the worms, as opposed to trying to dig them up from the garden. You can contact a local garden club or nursery; there are also several Internet sites that sell red worms.

Cardboard

Scissors

Four containers of the same size, four bricks, or four blocks of wood

Worm food (described in Step 9)

Directions

1. **With the help of an adult,** drill about twenty quarter-inch holes in the bottom of each bin.
2. Next, with an adult supervising, use a 1/16-inch bit to drill air holes on the sides of each bin. Your holes should be about an inch apart, and near the top edge of the bin.
3. With the same bit, drill about twenty-five holes in the lid of just one bin.
4. Soak the newspaper strips in a bucket or sink of water. Squeeze out the excess water—you want the newspaper to be moist, not wet.
5. Cover the bottom of one bin with moistened newspaper strips three or four inches thick. Mix in some dried leaves and a handful of soil (any type will do).
6. Release your worms into their new home.
7. Cut a piece of cardboard the size of the bottom of the bin. You will use this to cover the newspaper and soil. Moisten the cardboard the same way you did the newspaper. Place it gently on top of the newspaper strips, leaves, soil, and worms.

8. Using the undrilled lid for a tray, prop the bin up using either four containers of the same size, four bricks, or four blocks of wood. This allows excess moisture to drain out of the bin.

9. Feed your worms. Do not give them too much. Small amounts of food can be buried under the cardboard in different areas of the bin. Burying the food prevents fruit flies from becoming a problem. Worm food can include:

bread
grains
cereal
coffee grounds (and
    filters)
tea bags
vegetables, including
    peelings and rinds
fruits, including
    peelings, rinds,
    cores, and so on
grass clippings

Never feed worms meat, dairy products, eggs (eggshells are okay), or fats and oils.

10. After the first bin is full and food scraps are no longer recognizable, prepare the second bin the same way you did the first. Add food scraps. Place the second bin directly on the compost of the first bin. After a month or two, most of the worms will have moved to the second bin to get the food, and you can now use your first bin of compost in your garden. If you see worms still in the first bin, gently lift them up and transfer them into the second bin.

If your worms are dying or trying to get out, check to see if your bedding is too wet or too dry, and correct it. Make sure there is still enough bedding. If it looks as if it has been used up, add more bedding. If your bin smells, you may have added too much food, or there is too much moisture. Do not add food for a week or two if there is a lot in the bin, and make sure that enough air can flow through the bin.

Further Reading

Books

Bial, Raymond. *A Handful of Dirt*. New York: Walker Books for Young Readers, 2000.

Buczacki, Stefan and Beverley. *Young Gardener*. London: Frances Lincoln Children's Books, 2006.

Koontz, Robin. *Composting: Nature's Recyclers*. Minneapolis, Minn.: Picture Window Books, 2002.

Lovejoy, Sharon. *Roots, Shoots, Buckets & Boots*. New York: Workman Publishing, 1999.

Matthews, Clare. *How Does Your Garden Grow? Great Gardening for Green-Fingered Kids*. London: Hamlyn, 2005.

Rushing, Felder. *Dig, Plant, Grow: A Kid's Guide to Gardening*. Nashville, Tenn.: Cool Springs Press, 2004.

Winckler, Suzanne. *Planting the Seed: A Guide to Gardening*. Minneapolis, Minn.: Lerner Publications Company, 2002.

Works Consulted

Appelhof, Mary. *Worms Eat My Garbage: How to Set Up and Maintain a Worm Composting System*. Kalamazoo, Mich.: Flower Press, 1993.

Hamilton, Geoff. *The Organic Gardening Book*. New York: DK Publishing, 2004.

Marinelli, Janet. *The Environmental Gardener*. New York: Brooklyn Botanic Garden, 1992.

Stein, Sara. *Noah's Garden: Restoring the Ecology of Our Own Backyards*. Boston: Houghton Mifflin, 1993.

Tufts, Craig, and Peter Loewer. *The National Wildlife Federation's Guide to Gardening for Wildlife*. Emmaus, Penn.: Rodale Press, 1995.

On the Internet

Compost Guide: A Complete Guide to Composting
http://www.compostguide.com

I Can Garden
http://www.icaangarden.com/kidz.cfm

Kids Gardening
www.kidsgardening.org

Kids' Valley Garden
http://www.copper-tree.ca/garden/index.html

Organic Gardening
www.organicgardening.com

Organic Gardening Guru
http://www.organicgardeningguru.com/

Photo Credits: Cover, pp. 1, 2–3, 4–5, 6–7, 11, 12–13, 20–21, 30–31, 33, 36, 37, 38–39, 40—JupiterImages; p. 9—Felix Andrews/cc-by-sa-2.5; pp. 15, 17—Sharon Beck; pp. 22, 29, 35—Amie Jane Leavitt. Every effort has been made to locate all copyright holders of material used in this book. If any errors or omissions have occurred, corrections will be made in future editions of the book.

Glossary

algae (AL-jee)—Plantlike organisms that grow mostly in water.

annuals (AN-yoo-ulz)—Plants that live for a year or less.

biodegradable (by-oh-dee-GRAY-duh-bul)—A substance that can be decomposed, or broken down, by bacteria or other living things.

botanical garden (buh-TAN-ih-kul GAR-den)—A garden where plants are grown for exhibition and scientific study.

chemicals (KEH-mih-kulz)—Substances that have been prepared, usually artificially.

compost (KOM-pohst)—A mixture of decaying organic substances, such as dead leaves or manure, used for fertilizing soil.

decomposing (dee-kum-POH-zing)—Breaking down into basic parts.

ecosystem (EE-koh-sis-tem)—A collection of living things and the environment in which they live.

fertile (FER-tul)—Rich in material needed for plant growth.

fertilizers (FER-tuh-ly-zerz)—Materials that are spread on or worked into soil to help plants grow.

guano (GWAH-noh)—Animal droppings, especially from seabirds or bats, used in fertilizer.

herbicide (ER-bih-syd)—A substance used for killing plants, especially weeds.

insecticide (in-SEK-tih-syd)—A substance used for killing insects.

mulch—Organic matter such as leaves, wood chips, or compost spread on the ground around plants to prevent moisture from evaporating, add nutrients to the soil, and help prevent weed growth.

neutralizes (NOO-truh-ly-zez)—Makes something near either end of a scale go toward the middle.

nitrogen (NY-troh-jin)—A colorless, odorless gas that is found in the air and helps plants and animals grow; it is one ingredient in fertilizer.

nutrients (NOO-tree-untz)—Substances that keep living things healthy and help them grow.

organic (or-GAA-nik)—Something that comes from a living thing.

organism (OR-guh-nih-zum)—A living thing, such as a plant, animal, or bacteria.

perennials (per-EH-nee-ulz)—Plants that live for several years.

pollinating (PAH-lih-nay-ting)—When pollen is moved from one plant to another by any method, including wind and animals.

potpourri (poh-por-EE)—Mixture of dried flower petals or herbs used for fragrance.

vermiculture (VER-mih-kul-chur)—The use of specially bred earthworms to convert organic matter into compost.

Index